An introduction to the Stroudwater Navigation and the Thames & Severn Canal

ISBN No: 978-0-9561743-0-7
Published by the Cotswold Canals Trust, February 2009

Written by David Jowett and Richard Attwood
Compilation & Layout by David Jowett
Print Liaison: Sharon Kemmett at The Design Co-operative 01453 751778
Printed by AST 02920 497901

Front cover picture: From an old postcard of the Golden Valley, Chalford
Back cover photo: Coates Portal of Sapperton Tunnel
Photo on this page: St Cyr's Church at Stonehouse

www.cotswoldcanals.com

1

Contents

Introduction

The Cotswold Canals comprise the seven mile (12km) Stroudwater Navigation and the twenty-nine mile (46km) Thames & Severn Canal. The Stroudwater Navigation was opened in 1779 to link the River Severn with Stroud. Opened in 1789, the Thames & Severn Canal was built to connect the Stroudwater Navigation to the Thames at Inglesham creating a through route from the River Severn to London.

Following decline, abandonment and dereliction over many years, a society (now called the Cotswold Canals Trust) was formed in 1972 to protect and restore the canals. In July 2001, a feasibility report highlighted the benefits of a restored waterway. As a result, the two canals are being restored to their former glory by a partnership of organisations - more details can be found on pages 70 to 78.

This book has been produced by volunteers from the Cotswold Canals Trust to stimulate your interest in the canals, their history and the exciting future ahead.

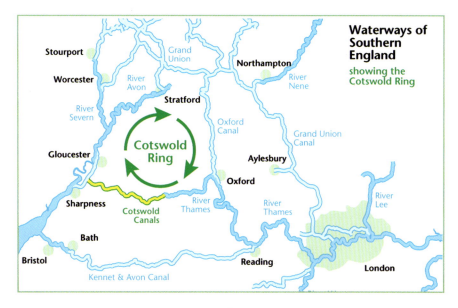

The Route

The Cotswold Canals weave their way through some of the most beautiful parts of the British Isles, in a landscape of hills, valleys and flowing water. The abundant mills once gave the area prime importance in the cloth industry and without them the canals would not have been built. A long distance footpath, *The Thames and Severn Way*, links the rivers Severn and Thames following as closely as possible the towpath of the Stroudwater Navigation and Thames & Severn Canal.

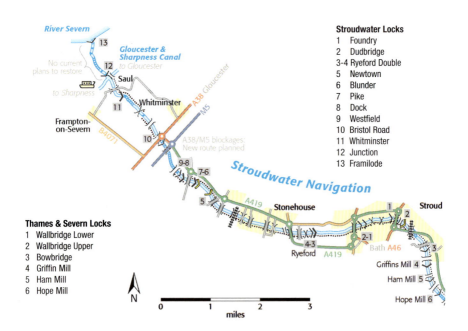

This footpath begins at Framilode Church on the banks of the River Severn, near the entrance to the Stroudwater Navigation and ends at Halfpenny Bridge, spanning the River Thames at Lechlade, just downstream from the end of the Thames & Severn Canal at Inglesham. Between these two rivers lie 36 miles of wonderful and contrasting scenery.

Leaving the River Severn's own long distance footpath, *The Severn Way*, the level farmland bordering the river gives way to a gentle rise in the land towards Stroud, past mills, former railway lines, hanging woods and rushing water in the shadow of the Cotswold edge.

The Stroudwater Navigation approaches Stroud's suburbs and finally the site of its terminal basin which was once found at Wallbridge in Stroud. This is where the Thames & Severn Canal begins, carrying on the cross-country route. It passes very close to the town centre before heading off to follow the winding valleys as it continues its slow climb to the summit level.

Key to Maps

Canal
in water
dry or reeded
infilled
towpath open

Locks
fully restored
structure restored
unrestored

Bridges
restored or intact
obstruction
site of swing-bridge

Round House

Trip-boat

Thames & Severn Locks		
1 Wallbridge Lower	8 Bourne	16 Valley
2 Wallbridge Upper	9 Beales	17-18 Bakers Mill
3 Bowbridge	10 St Mary's	19-20 Puck Mill
4 Griffin Mill	11 Iles Mill	21-22 Whitehall
5 Ham Mill	12 Ballinger's	23-24 Bathurst Meadow
6 Hope Mill	13 Chalford Chapel	25-26 Sickeridge Wood
7 Goughs Orchard	14 Bell	27 Daneway Basin
	15 Red Lion	28 Daneway Upper

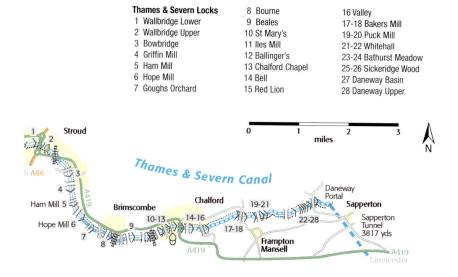

The 'alpine' village of Chalford marks the entrance to the Golden Valley - an autumn visit may give a clue to its name. Locks come thick and fast as the valley becomes ever steeper and narrower until, finally, the summit pound is reached at a height of 310 feet above sea level at Daneway.

The canal passes through the Cotswold Hills via historic Sapperton Tunnel but the *Thames and Severn Way* follows the paths that towing horses would have taken over the hills to the Coates portal. The tunnel was a wonder of its age when it was completed in 1789. A royal visit by King George III confirmed its importance. It was the longest canal tunnel at the time and still ranks as the third longest more than two hundred years after its construction. Just a mile along is the source of the River Thames which marks the end of the *Thames Long Distance Footpath*.

The route twists and turns along the contours of the summit level through open countryside and often over private land. It passes the old arm of the canal that extended into the heart of Cirencester and then begins a gradual descent into the Thames Valley through flights of locks at Siddington and South Cerney.

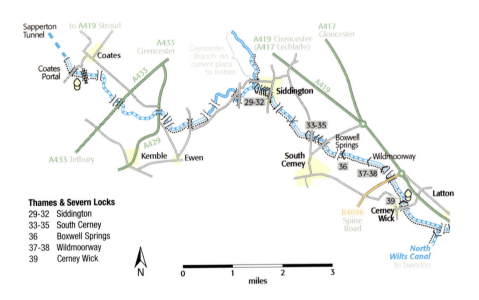

Thames & Severn Locks
29-32   Siddington
33-35   South Cerney
36   Boxwell Springs
37-38   Wildmoorway
39   Cerney Wick

The Cotswold Water Park has expanded in this area as worked-out gravel pits become lakes with water covering a surface greater than the Norfolk Broads. Latton Junction is the point at which the former North Wilts Canal left to wind its way round Cricklade to Swindon and via the Wilts & Berks Canal either to Abingdon on the Thames or Semington on the Kennet & Avon Canal. At Latton, the casual observer may ask how a restored canal would overcome the blockage created by

6

the new dual carriageway. Fortunately, after a long campaign, a hidden bridge was incorporated under the road in 1997 whilst it was being built close to the village of Latton. When restoration reaches this section of canal, this 'sleeping' navigable culvert will be brought into use.

At the other side of the new road, the route of the Thames & Severn Canal now passes through remote countryside as it heads towards the River Thames.

Key to Maps

Canal
≡ in water
▪▪▪ dry or reeded
▭▭▭ infilled
····· towpath open

Locks
⌃ fully restored
⌃ structure restored
⌃ unrestored

Bridges
= restored or intact
≍ obstruction
✕ site of swing-bridge

◗ **Round House**

⊞ **Trip-boat**

Thames & Severn Locks
39 Cerney Wick
40 Latton
41 Eysey
42-43 Dudgrove Double
44 Inglesham

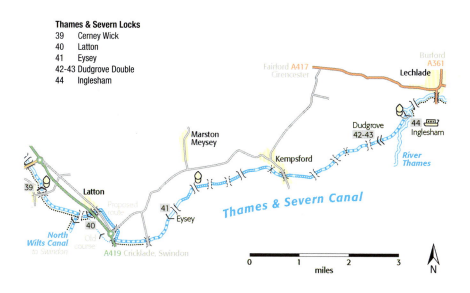

Once again on private land, the canal route passes Eisey Manor and nearby Marston Meysey before reaching the village of Kempsford which is close to the giant airfield at Fairford. Three more miles lead to the junction of the Thames where the last of five round houses overlooks the river at Inglesham, near Lechlade. This spot is best approached from Lechlade along the Thames-side path or better still, by boat!

History

There were many early attempts to build a navigation from the River Severn to Stroud. In the 1740s Richard Owen Cambridge built a man made waterway near Wheatenhurst for pleasure purposes. The Kemmett Canal was built between 1759 and 1763 from Framilode to the Stonehouse area. It featured the earliest known example of container traffic on an inland waterway.

The Stroudwater Navigation was built between 1775 and 1779 from Framilode, on the banks of the River Severn, to Wallbridge, Stroud. From the beginning, the canal was very profitable and a proposal was soon made for a link with the Thames and London. In 1781 a survey began of the line from Stroud to Cricklade on the River Thames which recommended the Stroud to Cirencester route. However, surveyor Robert Whitworth warned that trouble would be encountered on the summit which was to be built over "bad rocky ground". A Bill was introduced in 1783 and construction of the canal was expected to take six years. Josiah Clowes was appointed Resident Engineer. On 31st January 1785 the first vessel passed through the lock at Wallbridge in Stroud and went up the new canal as far as Chalford. The 241 feet rise from Wallbridge to the summit level at Daneway (near Sapperton) was completed in the summer of 1786 requiring 28 locks over a distance of seven miles.

At the summit came Sapperton Tunnel, the largest and longest canal tunnel built up to that time. Even to this day, its length has only been exceeded by two other canal tunnels in this country. It is 3817 yards long and about 14 feet wide by 15 feet high. Work on the tunnel started in 1784 and after problems with the difficult ground and an incompetent contractor, was completed in 1789. The first boat passed through the tunnel on the seven mile summit pound to Cirencester in April 1789.

Work had proceeded meanwhile to the eastern side of the summit where the canal descends 129 feet over 13 miles via 15 locks to the Thames. The first boat reached the River Thames at Inglesham Lock on 20th November 1789. Lack of experience in the design and construction of canals resulted in a shortage of water almost from the first day. Numerous locks were built to varying lifts and due to the narrowness

Above: Wallbridge   Below: Brimscombe Port.
Both pictures were painted by unknown artists in the late 1700s.
Reprinted courtesy of Stroud District (Cowle) Museum.

of the Golden Valley were constructed with intervening pounds of insufficient capacity. These problems, coupled with fissured limestone ground on the summit, made it wasteful of water. After using a wind pump for some years, the Company installed a Boulton & Watt single acting beam engine at Thames Head. In 1854 the Watt engine was replaced by a cornish beam engine of much higher capacity. The new engine could deliver three million gallons of water to the summit pound every 24 hours. The engine was scrapped in 1941 to aid the war effort.

The years 1820 to 1845 brought improvements to locks and constant maintenance kept leaks to a minimum. All locks between Chalford and South Cerney were shortened creating the characteristic double top gate recesses. Side ponds were added to some locks in the Golden Valley. The efficiency of the navigation was marked by steadily increasing receipts which peaked in 1841. However, competition from railways was growing and at the end of 1893 a notice was issued closing the canal east of Chalford until further notice. Despite protests the canal remained closed, but eventually led to the formation of a trust which took over the canal. The trust was formed by six other canal companies and five local authorities who reopened the canal throughout in March 1899. This achievement was short-lived as leakage on the summit caused the canal to close once again in June of that year.

In 1901 the canal was transferred to Gloucestershire County Council who began further restoration work. The length of canal from Cirencester to the River Thames was reopened in July 1902, from Stroud to Daneway in April 1903, and the summit pound in January 1904. The first vessel over the reopened summit was the *Staunch* in March 1904. The restored canal was still not completely reliable and was closed for at least twelve weeks of each year in 1905, 1906, and 1908 for repairs to the summit. It was also closed for twelve weeks in 1907 for repairs to Puck Mill Pound which was emptying in four hours through leaks in the clay puddle lining. The last loaded boat passed over the summit in May 1911 and only a few repairs were carried out in the next four years. In 1927 the canal was formally abandoned from Lechlade to Whitehall Bridge in the Golden Valley and in 1933 the remaining length to Stroud was also abandoned.

The Stroudwater Navigation, which had remained independent, carried on until 1941 when traffic of all kinds effectively ceased. It was abandoned by Act of Parliament in 1954 despite vigorous lobbying to keep it open by local figures, notably Mrs Enid Airey. The fifteen years following the abandonment of the Stroudwater were the most destructive period in its history. Sections of the Thames

Above: Thames Head Pump. Below: Entrance Basin at Framilode.

Both photos are from the early 1900s.

& Severn Canal, abandoned in the early part of the century had also become derelict. Sapperton Tunnel suffered one roof fall and two side falls. Short sections of canal were returned to agricultural use at the eastern end. Brimscombe Port was filled in and became an industrial estate. Construction of the M5 motorway and its link road to the A38 resulted in the loss of Bristol Road and Meadow Mill Locks and the one mile of canal linking them. A flood relief scheme by Severn Trent Water Authority merged the canal with the River Frome for about 400 yards and resulted in the infilling of Whitminster Lock. A total of nine swing bridges were fixed.

Over the years the remaining locks were allowed to decay with various service pipelines being installed at water level. British Rail enclosed the bridge over the canal at Stonehouse Court with an 'armco' tube and the road crossings at Stonehouse and Bath Road, Stroud were infilled. More recently, in 1987, the canal at Capel's Mill Viaduct was infilled to provide the Stroud East/West Bypass although a bridge was incorporated into the scheme to allow for restoration. The line of the canal is now protected in all District Council Local Plans.

In 1996 Gloucestershire County Council commissioned British Waterways to make a corridor study which would supplement the engineering studies which had already proved the feasibility of restoration. The resulting report examined the cost benefit of full or partial restoration and concluded that in either case the benefits to the local community were extremely good both in terms of payback and number of jobs created.

Ownership of the majority of the Stroudwater remained with the original company. After abandonment, Gloucestershire County Council sold much of the Thames & Severn east of Chalford to the riparian landowners. The Cotswold Canals Trust maintained good relations with many of these, including particularly the Bathurst Estate which owns a large section of the canal including Sapperton Tunnel.

The Cotswold Canals Trust, which had started out as the Stroudwater Canal Society in 1972, promoted a reversal of the destructive processes and undertook specific restoration works using not only local volunteer labour, but also the visiting Waterways Recovery Group and other organisations. The result of all this effort has been that most of the canal corridor was declared a Conservation Area.

Today, The Cotswold Canals Partnership is co-ordinating the restoration of these two beautiful canals, the first major project being the 'Phase 1A' section from Stonehouse to Brimscombe.

Above: Blunder Lock awaiting restoration in 1983.
Right: The plaque celebrates its restoration.
Below: The lock back in use in 2003.

BLUNDER LOCK
HIS ROYAL HIGHNESS
The Prince of Wales
re-opened this lock
on
Tuesday, 14th April, 1992

A Guide to the Cotswold Canals along the
Thames and Severn Way

This guide to the *Thames and Severn Way* will take the reader along the Stroudwater Navigation and the Thames & Severn Canal as closely as possible by following all the available towpath. Deviations to nearby roads and tracks will sometimes be required where it is difficult to walk along the canal route or where the route is in private ownership, especially in the east. Care should be taken not to stray on to land which is in private ownership.

The Cotswold Canals are subject to restoration, so it is likely that access will be improved and sections of canal will be restored after publication of this book. Where the *Thames and Severn Way* is subject to major changes during restoration, some passages describe the route 'before and after'.

The description of the route is 'not to scale' - the Stroud Valleys are packed with features whilst in the east the route is predominantly rural. Work to restore the Cotswold Canals has been concentrated in the west too, but it should be remembered that the stated aims of the Cotswold Canals Partnership include restoration of the whole route from Saul Junction to the River Thames.

This guide is useful for walkers to follow but much pleasure can also be derived by making an imaginary trip along the Cotswold Canals from an armchair! In either case, use of the appropriate maps will add to the appreciation of the journey.

Useful Maps

Ordnance Survey Landranger 1:50,000
162 Gloucester & Forest of Dean
163 Cheltenham & Cirencester

Ordnance Survey Explorer 1:25,000
168 Stroud, Tetbury & Malmesbury
169 Cirencester & Swindon
014 (covers short section of canal in west)

Map References
At some key points in this book, National Grid References are quoted. All of the maps listed here include instructions for reading the references under 'Technical Information'

Please check that you know which areas are covered before buying maps

Above: The former western entrance lock to the Stroudwater Navigation seen from the west bank of the River Severn in 2003.   Below: The eastern entrance to the Thames & Severn Canal at Inglesham, Lechlade in 1982.

Framilode to Saul

The starting point of the *Thames and Severn Way* can be found on the east bank of the River Severn at St. Peter's Church in Upper Framilode overlooking the River Severn. The *Severn Way* passes by along the river bank on its journey south towards the estuary (SO 751 104). The entrance lock to the Stroudwater Navigation is just out of sight to the north upstream.

The view along the Severn from this point is extensive and will vary according to the state of the tide. At quiet times the flow appears quite gentle, but after periods of heavy rain the water speeds past. At low tide, the muddy river bank on this side would not be tempting but some of the sand banks at the far side of the river look more inviting. The river should be be treated with great respect as the water can quickly surround and overwhelm these sand banks as the tide races in.

Setting off, the lane heads around the corner away from the river for around fifty yards to the site of Framilode Swingbridge which is now levelled. To the left of the old bridge, the infilled entrance basin from the River Severn can be glimpsed in what is now a private garden. The original lock into the river is still buried on the banks out of sight at the end of this garden but, if you are prepared to take a long drive via Gloucester, its heavy masonry entrance can be viewed from the west bank of the river on Rodley Sands. The structures on the Stroudwater Navigation were built to dimensions which would accommodate the type of boat common on the Severn in the late eighteenth century - the Severn Trow. The word Trow rhymes with crow deriving its name from a trough, the boat being flat-bottomed, so it could rest on Severn sandbanks. It usually had sails, so whilst it made its way towards Stroud and back, these could be removed and stored together with the mast in an old warehouse alongside the entrance basin.

Back on the site of the bridge, the towpath leads away past old cottages; residents of these dwellings once had to pay the canal company for the privilege of having windows overlooking their waterway. The canal is often reeded along this section although locals do endeavour to clear some reaches to maintain open water and encourage a mix of wildlife. One such section can be found around a hundred yards further on by the *Ship Inn* which is one of the few remaining canalside pubs along the Cotswold Canals.

A little further on is Moor Street Bridge (SO 752 100) and across the road the towpath continues. Eventually the canal ends but by continuing straight on with the

Above: The River Severn at Framilode between high tides on a calm day.

Below: The *Ship Inn* at Framilode by a section of canal cleared by local residents.

River Frome on the left (walking along the river bank, not on top of the flood defence) the cluster of buildings at Saul Junction can be seen in the distance. A variety of fences and stiles must be negotiated before passing a smaller group of buildings just before the junction. Until the 1960s these incorporated the canal-side pub, the *Drum and Monkey* which, like so many others, is now a private residence.

The reed-filled canal reappears on the right as Saul Junction comes into full view (SO 756 094). The lock to the west of the junction is notable for its unusual paddle gear which would be more at home on the Leeds & Liverpool Canal, two hundred miles to the north.

There are no plans to restore the Stroudwater between the River Severn and this point. The Gloucester - Sharpness Canal, which was built later than the Stroudwater forming this watery cross-roads, makes a more convenient connection to the national network of waterways. Finally completed in 1825 after many difficulties during construction, this Ship Canal once carried tall sailing ships from the Severn estuary at Sharpness to the heart of Gloucester. It locked down on to the Severn, by-passing the most treacherous reaches of this dangerous river. The canal is 16 miles long, originally had 16 bridges and is 16 feet deep. Saul is at the halfway point. Water is pumped into the canal at Gloucester and extracted at Purton, near Sharpness, to supply half of Bristol with drinking water.

Today, only the occasional load of freight passes this way. More common is the variety of pleasure boats, or perhaps the larger red and green boats belonging to the Willow Trust. These specially designed vessels are moored here when their volunteer crews are not giving people with disabilities the chance to get afloat.

Saul Junction is a rarity, being a canal crossroads on the level. Originally, the Stroudwater Navigation ran behind Junction House (home to the bridge-keeper) but the realignment was required when the newer ship canal was constructed. Once a 'secret place' that many locals had never discovered, Saul Junction is now a popular destination, especially on a sunny afternoon. What would a visitor in 2009 expect to find here? The new cafe a few hundred yards south along the towpath. A little closer, the 'Heritage Centre', with a canal shop and small exhibition about the canals' restoration, manned by volunteers from The Cotswold Canals Trust who also crew boat trips during the summer and at Christmas. Adding to the mix at this busy spot, and right on the waterway crossroads is a boatyard (R W Davis & Son) which specialises in construction of high-quality narrowboats. A dry dock occupies the corner of the boatyard nearest the junction.

Above: Saul Junction, 2006. 1. The Stroudwater heads east. 2. New marina site.
3. Boatyard and drydock. 4. The junction lock. 5. Original canal line.
Below: The rare sight of a commercial vessel at Saul in 2005.

The way across the Gloucester - Sharpness Ship Canal is over the pedestrian swing bridge which was only mechanised in recent years. The quarter mile section of the Stroudwater that follows is fully navigable and once offered tranquil moorings to members of Saul Junction Boat Owners Club. In 2008 they were joined by many more boaters who took advantage of the new 280 berth marina which was excavated from the low-lying land on the off-side.

At the end of the section, the canal was blocked in the 1960s. Once a swing-bridge, Walk Bridge (SO 758 089) was fixed after the canal was abandoned in 1954, but the structure is decaying and carries a weight restriction. It is planned to replace it with a high level fixed bridge.

Crossing the lane and continuing along the curving left bank of the Stroudwater Navigation, this open stretch of canal ends at Whitminster Lock. The structure was excavated in the mid 1990s by volunteers of the Cotswold Canals Trust in order to connect the canal into the River Frome. The waterways were realigned here in the 1970s, so the canal was lost, but the navigation will now join the river at this point to continue the navigation. The right bank of the River Frome should be followed, past the copse and underneath electricity lines, to the concrete farm bridge over the river.

By crossing the bridge the original towpath is rejoined alongside the Stroudwater Navigation. A short way ahead, the causeway across the canal was once Stonepits swing bridge. The towpath follows the canal south-eastwards for around half a mile, first past a large pipe that crosses the canal and then Occupation Bridge, a humpback bridge repaired in the 1990s by volunteers from the Cotswold Canals Trust. A Second World War pill box, part of Stopline Green, lies a little further along and then the busy A38 road (SO 773 074). The large group of buildings to the south along the driveway are Fromebridge Mill which is now a pub and restaurant.

The canal was infilled from here for around a mile when the M5 was built. Engineers have suggested several solutions to reinstate the canal through this area. Whichever route is chosen the new cut will rejoin the original line at Meadow Mill spill-weir which will be seen later.

The *Thames and Severn Way* temporarily leaves the line of the canal to pass the A38/M5 infilled section. A few yards up the hill from the A38 roundabout, and across the dual carriageway at the bottom of Whitminster Hill, is a footpath which

Above: 1. The Stroudwater. 2. Walk Bridge. 3. Complicated weir structures.
4. Whitminster Lock. 5. Whitminster House and Wheatenhurst Church.
Below: Close to the A38, the canal and Occupation Bridge

should be followed eastwards across the field. The path makes its way along the lower side of the wood called *The Grove* where bee hives are often found. The path curves up the slope to the left and follows the M5 motorway fence to the motorway bridge (SO 782 074). Crossing the bridge and following the lane for a third of a mile leads to Westend. Taking the field route (from SO 783 069) heading south leads to a crossing of the A419. Continuing straight on, the path emerges at Westfield Bridge and the Stroudwater Navigation (SO 781 063). Westfield Bridge is temporarily a 'bridge in a field' with Westfield Lock buried under the grass above. In high summer, the white strips of grass mark the walls of the main chamber which is the bottom lock of five in the Eastington Flight.

The path heads eastward across the small concrete bridge spanning Oldbury Brook to Meadow Mill spill-weir (SO 782 062). At one time Oldbury Brook flowed into the canal here, forming a large triangle of water, and out again over the spill-weir. This fascinating structure was uncovered from the undergrowth and restored by volunteers in the early 1990s. It was designed to allow the canal to be drained to several different levels. A boathouse here was the home of the canal company's ice-breaker. Immediately west of the spill-weir was a wharf from where coal was taken by horse and cart to woollen mills around Eastington and beyond.

The towpath now continues unbroken right to the summit level of The Thames & Severn Canal, many miles away. The next feature of note is Dock Lock and above here, a short way along the canal, lies Pike Bridge. The first bridge here was built in conventional brick but was later replaced by an attractive Edwardian structure. This too was dispensed with, the large chunks of rubble being consigned to the bottom of Dock Lock before its excavation and structural restoration (together with Pike Lock) in the early 1990s. In 2005, the Cotswold Canals Trust led a project to reconstruct the bridge you see today. Much of the old bridge was discovered under the infill and was preserved where possible whilst the load of the road is carried by new foundations behind the old brickwork. Across the road the towpath changes to the left hand side of the canal. The canal is now fully navigable from here for almost a mile and can be used by small craft thanks to the slipway at Eastington Wharf which was built by volunteers in 1992. Cotswold Canals Trust members have operated public boat trips from here.

The next lock within sight is the fully-restored Blunder Lock (SO 786 061). This was completed in 1992 and features a plaque on one balance beam that commemorates the reopening ceremony which was performed by Prince Charles on 14th April that year. The surrounding area was once the base for the Cotswold

22

Above: Eastington 2003, Meadow Mill Spill weir with Dock Lock in the distance

Below: Spring blossom in 2003 by Blunder Lock

Canal Trust's plant and equipment compound but is now pleasantly landscaped making it a popular spot for a picnic. Canal enthusiasts and others who have discovered this oasis often divert the half mile or so from the M5 to break long journeys by spending a few peaceful moments here.

A quarter of a mile further along is Newtown Lock, the first on either of the canals to be restored to full working order in 1991. This lifts boats to a gently curving length which passes below Newtown Roving Bridge (SO 791 055). The bridge is so named because it carries the towpath from one side of the canal to the other. A low level water pipe was removed from here in late 1993 thanks to Severn-Trent Water Board thereby opening up a further length of about 400 yards to navigation.

East of Newtown Roving Bridge, the land to the north of the canal was developed in 2007 and now accommodates industrial buildings but the view to the south begins to open up. A gently curving section leads to the world's first 'plastic' lifting bridge at Bond's Mill. The bridge carries a full Highways loading which is necessary because Bond's Mill Industrial Estate is down the slope from the canal. The bridge is electrically operated and really *is* constructed of reinforced glass fibre! Whilst problems have been experienced with some aspects of the bridge, the glass fibre element has not caused any trouble.

The circular building immediately to the north of the 'plastic' bridge is not one of the famous round houses but rather a gun turret built during the Second World War. Its function was to protect the industrial estate which made a valuable contribution to the war effort. A plaque on the tower celebrates the new bridge.

Leaving the bridge behind, the towpath makes its way along a high embankment for about 400 yards with views across to wooded hills making this a very pleasant stretch of waterway. The embankment was repaired in the mid 1980s after it had started to collapse down the hillside. Striding across the canal line ahead is a railway embankment through which the towpath passes although the canal has been culverted through a small six foot tube making this a major blockage.

At the other side of the bridge is a delightful scene. A wide expanse of water opens up. Known as 'The Ocean', there is some debate about whether this predated the canal as a pond, perhaps associated with Stonehouse Court, the large building behind the church a little further along which is now a hotel with a modern extension.

Above: Bonds Mill Bridge in 2005

Below: 'The Ocean' at Stonehouse in 2005

Restoration of the canal from here to Brimscombe, over six miles further on, became known as the Phase 1A scheme. Phase 1B takes in the canal route back from here to Saul Junction. The Phase 1A section should be the length where most changes will be seen whilst this edition of the book is on sale.

St Cyr's Church can be seen from the Ocean standing alongside the most picturesque, and perhaps most photographed, section of the Stroudwater Navigation with the land sweeping away below the canal and up again to the Cotswold Edge.

Nutshell Bridge is a most unusual structure with two houses clustered around, Nutshell House on the east side being the most distinctive. They have no recorded connection with the canal although they are linked by a passage under the bridge. There is no access on to the bridge from the towpath, but a short diversion on either side of the canal is well worth the effort to get a good view back to St Cyr's Church.

Housing developments now come closer to the canal on the outskirts of Stonehouse. Alongside the towpath are houses built in the 1960s whilst across the canal is a 1980s development. Further along on the off-side is another development from 2004 which has been built on the site of the old Midland Railway wharf. This lies alongside a new bridge from the year 1999 which was built as part of a road realignment scheme and removed a substantial blockage to the navigation.

A fixed bridge at an entrance to Upper Mills industrial estate is next. This former swing bridge will be replaced by a high level bridge. Just beyond is the building that was used by nearby Wycliffe School as a base for rowing and other water-related pursuits until a better home was found right by the junction at Saul. Next is an old railway skew bridge which crosses on unusual supports. This once carried the branch line from Stonehouse, through Dudbridge to a terminus at Nailsworth. Like many abandoned railway lines, it is now a popular cycle track.

Within a few yards is another major road crossing. Haywards Bridge, built in 1993, did not remove (or create) a blockage as this was a new canal crossing. Proof that the restoration project was credible came with the building of this substantial crossing of the canal to full navigable dimensions.

Above: Near Stonehouse in 2006 - 1. 'The Ocean'. 2. St Cyr's Church.
3. Nutshell Bridge. 4. Stonehouse Court Hotel.
Below: Wycliffe College Boathouse in the early 1900s from an old postcard.

Wycliffe College, Stonehouse, Glos Bathing in the Lower Field.

27

Another curving stretch leads to Ryeford Bridge (SO 814 046), from where the *Thames and Severn Way* shares the towpath with the *Cotswold Way* as far as the excellently restored Ebley Mill. The waterway remains wide and clear for around a third of a mile, thanks to dredging by the Canal Trust in the 1980s, and is much loved by anglers up to Ryeford Double Lock. A double lock combines two standard locks into one by sharing the bottom gates of the top lock with the top gates of the bottom lock. The top lock chamber off-side wall collapsed in the 1980s when a burst water main in the nearby road above caused water to cascade down the hillside. The subsequent surge of water was responsible for dumping several feet of silt into Blunder Lock which was passed some two miles back along the canal! The Company of Proprietors of the Stroudwater Navigation used compensation funds to rebuild the affected sections of this massive structure.

The cottage alongside Ryeford Double Lock has no road access but the peace was shattered here in the early 1990s when the Ebley Bypass was built at the bottom of the valley. The roar of cars can easily be heard and the road seen from the top of the lock.

The canal line above the lock is intact but about half a mile further on the canal was infilled in the 1960s. This allowed vehicle access to the local tip on the south side of the canal. Thankfully this is no longer in use and in 2007/8 the canal was excavated to Oil Mills Bridge (SO 826 046). The bridge was also reinstated to remove another levelled road crossing. The original abutments were revealed as the blockage was excavated and a new concrete decking was installed on piling made within the old abutments.

The stretch of canal through the bridge was excavated through a derelict industrial area in 2003. This was required of the developers who built the new 'Ebley Wharf' housing here. A new bridge, built of concrete but clad in bricks, leads around the back of Ebley Mill, an old woollen mill which was converted into offices for Stroud District Council. Being so tall, this is the most prominent building in the valley.

Soon after passing Ebley Mill the canal is diverted into the River Frome alongside although this arrangement will be changed to a long weir during restoration, breaking the direct link between canal and river. Hilly Orchard Bridge is a recently constructed metal structure close to more recently built housing. Until as recently as 1992, the next quarter mile of towpath was closed to the public which meant taking a lengthy diversion to rejoin the canal at Dudbridge where another modern bridge was built to navigable dimensions.

Above: Ebley in 2008. The canal had been infilled through an industrial site but was excavated by the developer who built the new houses.
Below: Ebley Mill by the River Frome in 2003. The canal is to the right.

Immediately to the east, two locks lift the canal to within a mile of Stroud town centre. The route is still surprisingly rural, passing alongside playing fields belonging to Marling School. Eventually, after passing two more fixed bridges that used to swing, old industrial buildings rise from the towpath. Green baize and yellow tennis balls are still made here. Cloth for army uniforms was also made here; going back to the early days of the canal, lengths of red cloth would be hung out to dry on nearby hillsides on tenterhooks which is the source of the saying we all know today.

The new Do-it-Yourself store Homebase towers over the end of the Stroudwater Navigation at Wallbridge. When opened, the Stroudwater had a terminus here, ending in a canal basin that is now infilled and has been home to various commercial users over the past years. Some original buildings remain. Stroud town centre stands up the hill from here.

The Thames & Severn Canal now begins. The path lies to the left and soon emerges at Wallbridge Lower Lock (SO 846 052). Beyond the lock, a little way along the path is a large building over the wall from the towpath which was originally the headquarters for the Company of Proprietors of the Stroudwater Navigation. From this position, a clear view of the old canal basin could be seen. The towpath emerges onto a busy A46 road which forms a blockage to navigation. As with so many such obstacles on this Phase 1A stretch (Stonehouse to Brimscombe), it is expected that the reader may encounter a busy scene of restoration or a newly completed bridge!

Wallbridge Middle Wharf lies below Wallbridge Upper Lock which was fully restored by the Stroud Valleys Project (with later help from the Cotswold Canals Trust) as a first step to revitalising this previously run-down area that forms the main gateway to visitors approaching Stroud from the M5 motorway. Until its demolition in the late 1980s, a bridge used to span the head of the lock. This was an old entrance into the Midland Railway station yard, Stroud's second station that competed with the Great Western Railway and its mainline station which survives in town close to this point. A fine example of a broad gauge railway goods shed also survives there waiting for a second lease of life.

Towering over the stretch of canal above the lock, the tall *Hill Paul* building deteriorated after it ceased to be used for the manufacture of clothing in the late 1980s. It was saved by a local pressure group and is now incorporated into a new development which is a great improvement on the previous dereliction.

Above: Wallbridge, Stroud, from the air in 2006.   1. Wallbridge Lower Lock.
2. Canal headquarters. 3. A46 road crossing. 4. Wallbridge Upper Lock.
Below: Wallbridge Upper Lock in 1986.

31

A quarter of a mile further on is the bridge under Dr. Newton's Way. The Cotswold Canals Trust was successful in fighting plans to infill a large section of canal when a by-pass was planned in the 1970s. An alternative route was constructed in 1987 to the south with lesser infilling and using the wide iron-spanned arch of the railway viaduct. The bridge which was incorporated under the new road provided an alternative for a diverted canal. It proved to be the first of many such bridges installed by Gloucestershire County Council on road improvement schemes, several of which have already been encountered. *Before restoration* through this area it is necessary to pass under the bridge and follow the signs to take the footpath under the railway viaduct and over the old rubbish tip to rejoin the towpath at the River Frome aqueduct. Plans will reinstate a canal route on a new line, so *after restoration* it is a simple matter of following the towpath. The imposing railway viaduct strides across the landscape launching trains on a long five mile climb up the valley, never far away from the canal.

From the aqueduct over the River Frome (SO 855 047), although close to Stroud, the towpath seems remote and rural but, either side of the site of Arundel Mill and the millpond that remains, more modern development borders the canal. Around a mile out of Stroud is Bowbridge Lock (SO 857 044) above which is the slightly older 'warehouse style' development that takes its name from the lock. Such was the dry state of this stretch of canal that it was let out for grazing before volunteers excavated by dragline and rewatered the canal in the early 1970s. Although the restoration society was then known as the Stroudwater Canal Society, for political reasons its first project was on the Thames & Severn Canal! Stanton's Bridge, just past the end of the Bowbridge Lock development, was repaired by volunteers too whilst Griffin Mill Lock also received attention. Just past the lock is the very attractive Jubilee Bridge which has required volunteer input over the years including rebuilding of the towpath-side wall in the mid 2000s. It is believed that this elegant lattice-work bridge was built and acquired its name during one of Queen Victoria's Jubilee years.

Continuing along the canal, which is still in water, Ham Mill Lock and its bridge are passed. Industrial buildings border the towpath, but across the canal the hills rise past the railway to Rodborough and Minchinhampton Commons. At intervals, paths come down the hillside to join the canal or cross to the valley bottom. These were used by workers who came down into the valley to work in the mills. One such path arrives over Bagpath Bridge which was subject to restoration in the 1970s.

Above: The canal in 1986 before the new road was built on its line

Below: Jubilee Bridge, east of Bowbridge shortly after refurbishment in 2003

Approaching Brimscombe, *before restoration*, the next landmark is a factory complex (SO 864 027). This factory site covers Hope Mill Lock and was once home to the *Abdella and Mitchell* boatyard where boats were built, often for export to places such as South America. Larger boats were built in sections and floated down to the Gloucester - Sharpness Canal. The canal is squeezed out leaving only the towpath for around a hundred yards but *after restoration* this short blockage should be removed. A short distance further on is Gough's Orchard Lock. As part of the Phase 1A restoration scheme, it was agreed that this could be a volunteer restoration project, to be undertaken mainly by visiting restoration groups such as the Waterway Recovery Group. The canal above here had been infilled for around a hundred yards in the 1960s as far as the *Ship Inn* at Brimscombe (SO 868 024).

By following the footpath signs straight across the road, The *Thames and Severn Way* now crosses the historic site of Brimscombe Port which was built as a massive trans-shipment depot. Locks from the River Severn to this point were built to accommodate trows - flat bottomed sailing vessels. The remainder of the route to the Thames provided for narrower, but longer, boats from the Thames, hence the need to provide for transfer of cargoes. The port also featured an island site which provided safe storage for goods including coal and a boat weighing machine which was used to gauge loads and thereby charge the correct tolls.

Before restoration, the route through the port is not straightforward. From the *Ship Inn* the road should be crossed and the factory road followed for a short way before taking the footpath on the left for a few yards to the A419 opposite the Brimscombe shops. After another few yards heading eastwards, a right turn should be taken on to the next footpath which emerges into the site of Brimscombe Port alongside the office entrance to an unoccupied large factory building. Note the plaque attached to the building which records that this site is the former Brimscombe Port. A plate from a milepost can also be found on the factory wall. A route should be taken across the car parking area towards the hillside and the main road exit. Just before the bridge, the path to the east should be taken with the River Frome to the right, walking away from the old mill buildings. Over the next few hundred yards the road becomes a footpath, with the river to the right, along the edge of the old port walls and emerges at Bourne Lock (SO 873 022). The old port wall has been restored to its former glory by the Waterways Trust.

During restoration of the port site, direction signs will be in evidence and should be followed and *after restoration* it should be easier to pass through the port and along to Bourne Lock.

Above: An attractive corner of Brimscombe Port in 2005 - the isolated
Salt Warehouse on the right is the only original port building to survive
Below: Mileplate at Brimscombe Port and milestone near Chalford in 2006

Bourne Lock is a dimensional one-off, built 90 feet long and just over 16 feet wide. The old buildings by the lock were rescued from dereliction by a local businessman who restored them and brought his *Noah's Ark* cycle business here from a premises it had outgrown in Chalford. A substantial obstacle to navigation above the lock is encountered where the railway crosses over as it continues its steep climb to the summit. A towpath is maintained under the railway, where the one-time bridge has been infilled. After negotiating the gloomy railway arch the area on the off-side once accommodated the canal company's boatyard; this is why the previous lock was wider to allow passage of Severn trows to the yard. The curving towpath reaches Beales Lock. Until the 1960s, Brimscombe Station could be found here near the railway crossing together with sheds for the bankers, the engines that would help pull some trains up to Sapperton Railway Tunnel.

A pretty stretch leads to St Mary's Lock (SO 887 023) which takes its name from nearby St Mary's Mill. It is worth diverting for a few minutes up the steep steps on the eastern side of the bridge to the railway crossing at the former St Mary's Halt which towers above the lock. Because the crossing is listed, it cannot be automated so is still manned. The embankment blocking navigation at the head of the lock was once spanned by a massive wooden viaduct designed in 1845 by the great Victorian Engineer Isambard Kingdom Brunel as part of the Cheltenham and Great Western Union Railway.

After passing under this second major blockage, caused once again by an old bridge being filled in, the towpath continues to Iles Lock and then to an infilled Ballingers Lock, which has a row of garages built on it. The green paddle gear by the garages was designed and built by volunteers from the Cotswold Canals Trust. The towpath lies alongside a narrowed but dredged channel to Chalford Round House (SO 893 025). This is the first of five round houses along the canal which are described in more detail in their own chapter. The plate from a milepost can be seen across the dredged canal above the culvert leading into the canal opposite the round house.

Towering over the Chalford Wharf area up on the road is Christ Church. This is perhaps the best place to view the next feature of note. The wall facing the road of the first building past the culvert carries the faint remains of an old painted advertisement which reads "James Smart.... Boats, Barges...." Passing below the James Smart advert the canal disappears and only the towpath remains

Above: Brimscombe Station near Beales Lock in the early 1960s
- the engine is a Collett Class 1P 0-4-2T
Below: Ballingers Lock, Chalford with Round House in background - early 1900s

Stroud Valley. Chalford.

following road widening in the 1950s. Chapel Lock lies buried in a grass verge. The towpath now lies between a narrowed canal channel and the boundary wall of the one-time Bliss Mills complex. The copious springs flowing into the canal in this area are part of what is known locally as the 'Black Gutter'. The buildings across the channel house the *Chalford Chairs* factory and a shop with small car park where the canal curves round to the crossing of the A419.

Bell Bridge is long gone, but engineers have solutions for its reinstatement. The head of Bell Lock can still be seen although the rest of the lock chamber was filled in as part of the Cowcombe Hill road widening and straightening in the 1930s.

There now follows the most popular length of the route as it enters the Golden Valley. All through the year, but especially on autumn Sundays, walkers park their cars here and make their way up the beautiful valley to the pub at the top. After a refreshing break they make their way back again! The scenery changes as the valley sides close in with houses clinging to the sides of the steep hills. Another canal-side pub, The *Red Lion*, has its own connection to the towpath by a short bridge across the River Frome. The towpath winds its way along the valley bottom, past Clowes Bridge (named after a canal engineer) and Red Lion Lock. The track over the bridge and up the hillside was closed by the building of the railway which is built into the hillside on what appear to be half viaducts. The top of the off-side bottom quoin has carved in it the inscription dedicated to the stonemason who built this lock - 'Herbert Stansfield, 4 December 1784'.

The canal now clings to the edge of the valley to avoid what was once the millpond of Sevilles Mill and is now usually patrolled by a flock of geese. Like the millpond, the mill has also vanished. The canal becomes wide and reedy and is fed by more outflows of the Black Gutter. Valley Lock was partially restored by volunteers from the Waterway Recovery Group and lies above a mill leat which is now the main course of the River Frome. The remains of the mill culverts and the circular marks made by a water wheel can be seen just below the lock. The large building close to the lock was once a public house, and until its closure the last name it adopted was the *Valley Inn*.

All locks from Valley Lock, over the summit, to Wildmoorway Lower Lock were shortened soon after the canal was opened to save water. They were shortened by building new top gate recesses over an arched extension to the top cill (the actual step in the lock which is usually just below the top lock gates). These features are unique to the Thames & Severn Canal.

Above: Close to the round house at Chalford in the early 1900s
Below: Valley Lock in 2006. 1. Former *Valley Inn*. 2. Valley Lock partially
restored. 3. The spill weir had been filled in but was excavated by volunteers

Perhaps this is the most scenic length of the Cotswold Canals and it is certainly the most heavily locked. Leaving Valley Lock behind, the canal curves gently to the left until it reaches a large brick building on the off-side which was built in the late 1800s to house Chalford Waterworks. This makes a useful landmark because it is opposite this building that a milestone can be found at the edge of the towpath. Although some of the original plates that were attached to the stones have been accounted for, most were lost or stolen by souvenir-hunters. Several can be found at relocated sites, such as the ones already noted at Brimscombe and Chalford. Here at Chalford, a replica mileplate was installed in 2002

The towpath surroundings become increasingly wooded along the next third of a mile approaching Baker's Mill with the amount of water in the canal varying according to the season. Towards the end of this stretch, the canal was lined with concrete during major restoration works in the early 1900s. Locals came to know this area as 'The Conk' for obvious reasons. A large expanse of water that opens up on the left was built as a reservoir for the canal but is now a private lake. As the valley closes in again, the canal bed is mainly dry as the frequency of ungated locks increases. In the next two miles come Puck Mill Locks (SO 921 029), Whitehall Locks, Bathursts Meadow Lock, Siccaridge Wood Locks and finally the summit is reached at Daneway Locks. Some of the locks through Siccaridge Wood feature side ponds which curve away from the top of each lock and around the sides. This mechanism allowed for the storage of more water between the locks that were especially closely spaced.

It may be difficult to see through the foliage, but between the top two locks is an entrance to Daneway Basin. This formed a temporary terminus during the construction period of the canal and more especially Sapperton Tunnel. A better view can be had from the road which crosses the canal. The bridge here was under threat in the 1970s but was quickly listed and saved. Across the road is a welcome 'canal-side' pub which was previously mentioned as the destination for those walkers that had parked at Chalford.

Previously known as the *Bricklayers Arms*, the *Daneway Inn* was built around the same time as the canal and was initially occupied by the navvies of the day who worked on the canal and especially the nearby tunnel. The pub car park is sited on the infilled top lock, (SO 939 034) which marks the start of the summit pound at 310 feet above sea level.

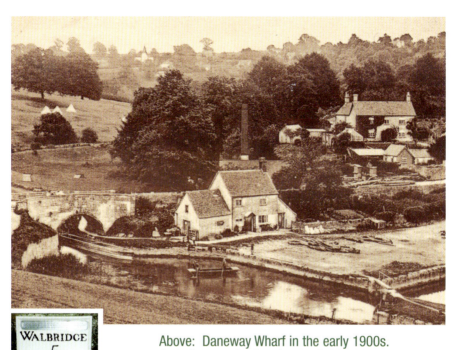

WALBRIDGE
5
INGLESHAM
23¾

Above: Daneway Wharf in the early 1900s.
Left: A new mileplate for the Golden Valley
Below: The Daneway Inn in 2005 from the canal bridge.

41

The level towpath winds along the hillside to the Daneway Portal of Sapperton Tunnel (SO 944 034). This one-time Gothic structure was restored to its former glory in 1996 by stone masons commissioned by the Cotswold Canals Trust and English Heritage. Sapperton Tunnel is described in more detail elsewhere in this book. Needless to say, this impressive feat of engineering was a wonder of the age when it was opened in 1789. The rubble which is encountered alongside the towpath about fifty yards from the portal is the remains of a cottage which was still occupied in the 1960s. Theft and vandalism led to its unfortunate demise.

The route across the top of the tunnel is best followed with the aid of an Ordnance Survey map. In any case, there is no pedestrian way through the tunnel so *The Thames and Severn Way* passes above the portal and diagonally up across the field towards Sapperton village, following the route taken by the horses. The field path turns into an upwards path between the cottages. At the road a left turn is made towards St Kenelms Church and then right at the church up the lane past the *Bell Inn*. Following the lane out of the village, a right turn is taken and after 100 yards a left at the cross roads. The clumps of beech trees on top of small mounds mark construction shafts to the canal tunnel below. These shafts are capped by rotting timber and earth covers. They are very dangerous so *THESE MOUNDS SHOULD NOT BE INVESTIGATED.*

The road is followed for just over half a mile and then a path is taken downwards across the field on the right. Crossing the A419 (SO 957 020) and, following the path across the opposite field, Hailey Woods is entered. Following the track through the wood and passing through the bridge under 'God's Wonderful Railway' - the old Great Western Railway line - (SO 965 010) the path emerges at the *Tunnel House Inn* and the Coates Portal (SO 956 006). The portal is a magnificent classical structure restored by a stonemason commissioned by the Canal Trust in 1977. The *Tunnel House Inn* close to the portal was once a three storey building until a fire gutted the structure in 1952. The pub was rebuilt some years later, one storey short.

Walking away from the tunnel, the towpath stretches along 'Kings Reach'. King George III made a visit here whilst staying at nearby Cheltenham in 1788 and was suitably impressed by what he saw. Tarlton road bridge is a high crossing and, once through, the towpath climbs so that it is high above the canal and level with the road bridge.

Above: The entrance to Sapperton Tunnel at Daneway in the early 1900s
Below: The Tunnel House Inn in the early 1900s. The building had three storeys
before a fire in 1952 and rebuilding to two storeys, years later.

After a few hundred yards Coates Round House appears out of the trees. Although in private ownership, the round house was rescued from dereliction by the Cotswold Canals Trust but only after it had lost its inverted conical roof. The canal is narrowed at this point which enabled the previous section to be isolated by inserting lengths of wood known as stop planks. The railway is encountered once again but this time on a fine, high skew bridge. It is worth taking a few minutes to admire the arch brickwork before walking the quarter of a mile to Coatesfield (sometimes called Trewsbury) Bridge (SO 978 001).

For the first time since the M5, the towpath now ceases to be a public right of way. By turning right from the towpath onto the bridge a path can be followed down a lane to a field. Following the path across two fields, the source of the River Thames is soon reached (ST 995 981). A visit to this area in a wet winter will show that whilst this place is the official source of the River Thames, the actual source of the river are the springs inside Sapperton Tunnel which reach this point via a leaky canal above the 'source'! After retirement from a London Exhibition, a statue of Old Father Thames was installed here but was relocated to St John's Lock at Lechlade after vandalism took its toll. A simple stone complete with inscription took its place.

Continuing across two more fields, with the canal hidden in the trees to the left, the path joins the A433 Cirencester to Tetbury road. By turning left along the road the canal is crossed at Thames Head Bridge. A pumping station was built close to here just to the south to deliver much needed water to this summit level. At the next cross roads a right turn is taken for around half a mile to Smerrill and the A429 road. Just before Smerrill the remains of the Smerrill aqueduct embankment appear on the right (ST 998 988). At the A429, the embankment resumes on the opposite side of the road. Long after the canal was abandoned, the road was realigned at a higher level after removal of a large section of the embankment. After turning right along the road up the incline the next left turn is taken along the lane to Ewen. Passing under the old Cirencester branch line rail bridge at Ewen Wharf (SU 001 985) the canal is on the left with Halfway Bridge hidden amongst the trees just after the railway bridge.

A track on the left leads to Halfway Bridge, so named as it is halfway between Stroud and Lechlade. This was restored in the late 1990s to preserve a rarity on the Thames & Severn. After the canal was abandoned many humpback bridges were demolished as part of a 'job creation' scheme during the Depression of the early 1930s. Steps on the left side of the bridge lead down to the towpath. Thanks

Above: A visiting group at Coates Round House in 2007
Below: In the early 1960s shortly after road widening, the profile of the canal in the Smerrill embankment can be seen clearly.

to the local landowner, the towpath is a 'permissive' path for the next half mile or so. At the height of summer, the path may be overgrown, so the road may be followed instead. At Park Leaze (SU 006 985) there was once a humpback bridge but the lane here should be crossed and the towpath followed until it rejoins the nearby lane.

The lane is followed towards Siddington because the canal has become a grassy field. After around half a mile, and shortly after passing beneath electricity pylons, on the left is a stile in the hedge (SU 015 990). The path from here may be followed across the field to Bluehouse Farm, which was once a lengthsman's cottage. From Bluehouse Farm the canal follows the contour in huge sweeping curves on an embankment to Siddington top lock. Turning right down the track to rejoin the lane, the canal crosses the lane about 50 yards before the road junction. Turning left at the Somerford Keynes road there is a right turning after 50 yards to Siddington. At the playing field a right turn leads along the lane to the humpback bridge at the top of the Siddington flight of locks (SU 031 996).

Just before the top lock is the junction with the former Cirencester Arm, which is now a private garden. As an optional diversion, the Cirencester Arm may be followed along the field edge behind Pound Close. For a short distance the forlorn remains of the canal channel can be seen before the Love Lane industrial estate removes all traces of the canal. The line of the canal runs under a supermarket, the bypass and a housing estate. The basin at the end of the arm is marked by Whitworth Road, in honour of Robert Whitworth who built the canal.

Back at Siddington the *Thames and Severn Way* now follows the towpath once again as far as Cricklade.

From the humpback bridge, the towpath lies alongside the first locks on the long, gentle descent towards the River Thames. This area was subject to extensive landscaping works by volunteers in the mid 1990s. The last of four locks has been replaced by a house which presents a challenge for future restoration. However, the towpath still passes by this spot and this crosses the Ashton Keynes road close to the *Greyhound* pub. The canal is now just about in water, although crossed by two farm causeways. It remains this way until Cowground Bridge is reached (SU 037 992). Cowground Bridge is one more of the few remaining humpback bridges on the eastern half of the Cotswold Canals, one that wasn't destroyed as part of that job creation scheme during the Depression. The towpath now leads on to cross the ancient water meadows of the River Churn.

Above: Halfway Bridge near Ewen

Below: Siddington top lock is through the bridge

47

The canal emerges from its enclosing hedges to a much more open aspect across level meadows. Directly ahead across the meadows is the River Churn. In the 16th century a system of water channels was created here fed by temporary wooden dams at stone abutments built into the river course. The diverted water was allowed to flood the meadows during the winter months to prevent the grass from freezing and encourage the growth of an early crop of grass for the sheep which were grazed there. This process was often repeated a number of times during the year. When the canal was constructed, culverts were built under the low embankment to allow the practice of flooding the water meadows to continue.

The embankment across the water meadows leads to the foot bridge over the River Churn. The earth embankment which carried the canal over the culverted river was blown up during the Second World War by the Home Guard as an exercise. This section of towpath was unusable, until the 1990s when the Ramblers Association and County Footpaths Department erected the wooden foot bridge. The towpath is followed with glimpses of the winding River Churn through the trees to the right. The canal enters a deep cutting, with a new golf course on the off-side. Until the 1990s the towpath had all but disappeared but a mix of locals and visiting volunteer groups created a new level path which emerges at the top lock of the South Cerney flight (SU 046 983). The lock is infilled and is cultivated by the owner of this and the old lock-keeper's house.

Crossing the road, the canal appears to have vanished. The *Thames and Severn Way* follows the footpath along the line of the canal diagonally to the right across the field. Buried in this field are two locks and during dry summer months the outline of the circular pounds and lock chamber walls can still be seen. Old photographs show the canal across this field bordered by a dry-stone wall, hedge and mature trees. The next road crossing at Northmoor Lane (SU 052 982) leads to a four mile section of canal which is mainly intact, though usually without water, and has received much attention from restorers over the last 30 years. Volunteers from the Cotswold Canals Trust, the Dig Deep Organisation and the Waterways Recovery Group have all played their part.

The canal gently winds its way towards Bow Wow Lane, South Cerney, and the site of Crane Bridge. Soon after is Boxwell Springs Lock (SU 057 977) which was structurally restored by the Waterway Recovery Group in the mid 1990s. The stop planks which impound the water above the lock will be replaced by lock gates

Above: The outline of the infilled South Cerney top lock can be seen clearly

Below: Repairing Boxwell Springs Lock in the mid 1990s

when the canal is ready for full navigation. Away to the right are the first signs of the Cotswold Water Park lakes which border the canal for the next two miles.

The gradual descent towards the Thames continues, through Upper Wildmoorway Lock, sometimes known as Humpback Lock, to Lower Wildmoorway Lock (SU 072 973). This lock is unique in having a side pond designed to save water during the operation of the lock. The side pond can be seen next to the towpath as it passes the lock chamber. The house which stands right on the lockside was rebuilt in recent years after the original structure became derelict to the stage of having only one wall standing. The lock has been structurally restored (together with the bridge here) and the canal between the lock and the Spine Road was fully dredged as part of a major canal restoration event known as Dig '95. Six hundred volunteers spent a weekend working on locks, clearing towpaths and generally improving the canal-side environment.

Until 2004, the *Thames and Severn Way* was blocked by Spine Road which was built to allow removal of gravel thereby creating the Water Park. Funding was unexpectedly obtained to remove this blockage by building a new navigable bridge. Decorative stainless steel features portray reeds and bulrushes on this important gateway to the Cotswold Water Park. The new bridge allows walkers to negotiate the dangerous road in safety. The towpath then passes the Water Park 'Gateway' Centre complete with a welcome cafe. New development is now in evidence and the nearest lakes in the Water Park are surrounded by houses and a hotel. Along the next mile or so, the A419 road can be heard and often seen detracting from the otherwise rural towpath. The next feature of note is Cerney Wick Lock which has its own round house (SU 078 960). The lock was restored by volunteers from the Cotswold Canals Trust in the early 1980s and makeshift top gates were installed. The *Crown Inn* is within sight along the lane to Cerney Wick. Crossing the road, the *Thames and Severn Way* continues for another mile to the site of Latton Junction (SU 087 954).

The junction is with the North Wilts Canal, also subject to restoration plans, as is the Wilts & Berks Canal which it joins at Swindon. It is likely that a restored North Wilts Canal would join at a different location but this has not deterred volunteers from both the Wilts & Berks Canal Trust and the Cotswold Canals Trust from working at Latton Junction which is usually in water. The North Wilts left to the south-east under a bridge and crossed the nearby leat by means of a small aqueduct into Latton Basin. The house here is now a private residence, but a public footpath passes behind the house where the North Wilts Canal's towpath can be followed.

Above: Wildmoorway Lower Lock with partially rebuilt cottage in 2005

Below: Newly restored Spine Road Bridge in 2005

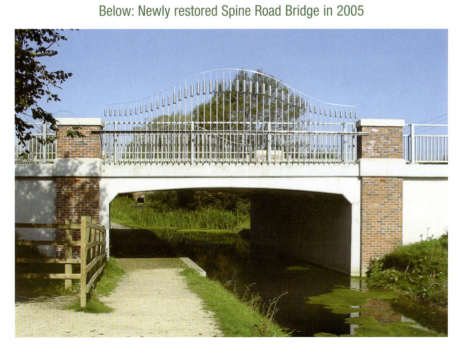

Back on the mainline, the *Thames and Severn Way* now reverts to a public footpath crossing the lane and following the north bank of the River Churn. The shallow depression to the left is the canal. The canal depression vanishes and the footpath swings to the left across the field to the far corner and the A419 (SU 093 953). The footpath should be followed towards Cricklade and on to the old road for around half a mile eventually arriving at the former Cricklade wharf house (SU 099 945).

When it was built in 1997 the major road here could have created a serious blockage. However, after protracted protesting, lobbying and with the help of Gloucestershire County Council, a navigable culvert was incorporated under the road. Today, it is very difficult to see but is full of gravel and waiting for restoration of this section when it will awake from its slumbers.

Turning left the bridge across the A419 should be taken. By following the road verge for 100 yards to the right and turning left, over two stiles, the dry canal channel can be rejoined as the towpath of the Thames & Severn Canal.

The towpath should be followed for half a mile on the low embankment and across Ampney Brook. The towpath on the embankment over the brook and for the next 200 yards has vanished. The *Thames and Severn Way* follows the bank of the brook for a few yards and then proceeds along the unsurfaced track east towards Eisey Manor. The entrance drive to the manor is flanked by two canal mileposts, complete with distance plates removed when the canal was partly infilled.

Between here and the end of the Thames & Severn Canal there is now very little of the remaining towpath which is a public right of way. By using the appropriate Ordnance Survey maps, a variety of routes to Lechlade may be chosen. What follows is one suggestion.

Walking away from the manor, the infilled canal is crossed where once there was a humpback bridge. After half a mile the Kempsford road is reached. A right turn should be taken and the road followed for a little more than a mile. One hundred yards past the left hand turning to Marston Meysey a track (SU 132 965) leads towards Marston Meysey Round House and its modern addition. Just before the round house is a left turn over a stile and a track which skirts the boundary of the round house. The track turns sharp right onto the infilled canal bed. The infilling took place so long ago that there is now no visible trace of the canal.

52

Above: Building a bridge under the new Latton Bypass in 1997

Below: Cricklade Wharf House in 2004

Climbing over the stile and heading east along the rough ground, which was the canal, the path passes between field fences. The edge of the next field should be followed and at the field corner the route bears left for twenty or so yards to the entrance into the next field. The canal line continues ahead bearing to the left towards the distant hedge and the former Crooked Bridge.

The *Thames and Severn Way* bears slightly to the right straight across the field to the drive leading to the Second Chance Caravan Park. The way ahead is left along the drive to the lane. Up the lane around one hundred yards on at its highest point is the site of Crooked Bridge which once crossed the canal at a sharp angle, hence the name. The lane should be followed to the Kempsford road where a right turn should be taken.

After half a mile, Oatlands Bridge can be spotted to the right down a short track (SU148 968). The bridge is in excellent condition although the canal, which was on a slight embankment, has been totally ploughed out of existence. There is a brick built into one of the parapets which has the words 'Stonehouse Brick Company' cast into it. The bricks for this bridge and probably other buildings in the area were brought by boat all the way from Stonehouse.

The road should be followed towards Kempsford and then a right turn, past the *Anchor Inn*, into the village. Continuing through the village for half a mile, the site of the canal crossing is reached at Kempsford Bridge (SU 161 967). The canal only exists as a grassy strip and stables. Just before the crossing a left turn should be taken along Ham Lane. The road turns into a gravel track leading to a junction of tracks and footpaths. Turning right the gravel workings should be on the left. Where the track rises and the gravel workings end is the site of Green Lane Bridge. By continuing, Hannington Lane can be joined (SU 168 964).

The final section of the *Thames and Severn Way* has to follow the *Thames Path* as there are no public footpaths following the route of the canal. The delights of the canal passing Brazen Church Hill and of Dudgrove Double Lock must remain a secret for the time being.

The lane should be followed, over the River Thames at Hannington Bridge, and after 200 yards a left turn is taken along a metalled track. After 100 yards, just before the entrance to a house, the bridle path on the right should be followed for around a mile. Eventually a stream is crossed by a footbridge. After 100 yards the hedge line should be followed to the right to Upper Inglesham (SO/195965).

Above: Oatlands Bridge in 1996

Below: The River Thames and church at Kempsford from an old postcard

There now follows an unpleasant mile and a half northwards along the fast and busy A361 towards Lechlade. A left turn is made along the lane to Inglesham Church (SU 205 985). The field on the right is the site of the mediaeval Inglesham village. Just before the houses, the stile on the right should be climbed and the backs of the gardens followed to the River Thames. The river bank should be followed to the end of the Thames & Severn Canal (SU 205 988) and its confluence with the River Coln and the River Thames. The footbridge over the river is a good viewpoint for the end of the canal and its round house hidden amongst the reeds and weeping willows. This point on the River Thames is acknowledged to be the limit of navigation for most boats.

The river bank should be followed for nearly a mile. If this is a summer weekend, the Cotswold Canals Trust trip boat *Inglesham* may be available for short trips. At other times it is available for charters. The trips depart from the riverside car park (SU 212 994) within sight of Halfpenny Bridge in Lechlade which marks the end of the *Thames and Severn Way*.

The view from the River Thames. The round house is on the left and the entrance lock is on the other side of the bridge.

Above: Cotswold Canals Trust's trip boat *Inglesham* departs from the riverside at
Lechlade and turns here by the entrance to the Thames & Severn Canal.
Below: The trip boat at Halfpenny Bridge, Lechlade.

Sapperton Tunnel

The building of Sapperton Tunnel on the Thames & Severn Canal was the greatest single achievement in the construction of the Cotswold Canals. At 3,817 yards long (over two miles), it was the longest canal tunnel in the country when built. Today it is still the third longest ever built in this country.

The builders dug shafts down from the surface which was 200 feet above in places. When the proposed line was reached they proceeded to bore their way from the bottom of one shaft to the next until the 'primary headway' was completed. This was opened out and lined with brick or left as bare rock. Even today the rock clearly bears the marks of their tools and drill holes where lumps were blasted away.

Work in 1982 to retrieve fallen portal masonry at Daneway

Above: The restored western portal at Daneway in 2003.

Below: A mix of brick-lined and unlined inside the tunnel.

King George III was suitably impressed when he came to see the tunnel in 1788 during a stay in nearby Cheltenham. The stretch of canal outside the tunnel at Coates accordingly became known as 'King's Reach'. The tunnel took five years to complete and on its opening in 1789 boats were able to navigate inland between the Rivers Severn and Thames for the first time.

Trade on the canal declined in the mid nineteenth century and the last recorded passage of the tunnel was made in 1911 after which the cross country waterway link was progressively abandoned between 1927 and 1954. Falls occurred at the western end of the tunnel where it passed through Fullers Earth.

The portals crumbled into the canal but the Canal Trust financed restoration of the eastern Coates Portal. The grand reopening was performed by Lord Bathurst in 1977 and nineteen years later, his son, Lord Apsley, was kind enough to do the same at the newly restored western castellated Daneway Portal. This isolated structure had suffered from vandalism over the years and the stonemasons were able to retrieve most of the masonry from the canal bed.

Coates portal in 1976, after clearance of vegetation but before restoration

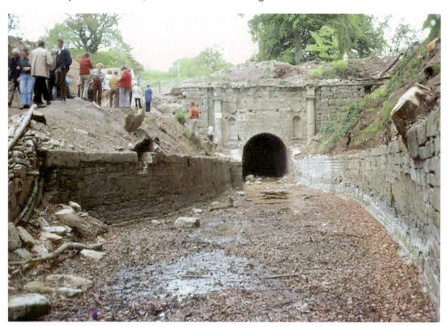

Above: Coates portal in 1976, during restoration.
Right: The restoration target board in 1976.
Below: In pristine condition shortly after completion.

Round houses

The Cotswold Canals are well-known for the five unusual round buildings that were constructed along the Thames & Severn Canal shortly after the canal was opened. There are no records to show why they were built this way. Only two were built alongside a lock, so they were never lock-keeper's houses but rather lengthsmen's dwellings. The Stroudwater Canal Company had not built anything of this nature ten years earlier.

Two local buildings may provide a clue to their origin. A round folly can be found alongside the road between Siddington and South Cerney near Cirencester although this has small turrets. A structure that bears a closer resemblance is an old teasel-drying house which lies just off the A46 road at Woodchester, two miles south of Stroud.

The two round houses at Chalford and Cerney Wick were built with normal conical roofs which is the logical way to top off a circular building. However, the remaining three at Coates, Marston Meysey and Inglesham featured unusual funnel-shaped roofs. These round houses were in more remote locations and the strange design provided a cunning way of catching rainwater to channel down to underground tanks. Conventional hand-pumps were then used to retrieve the water.

The ground floor was intended to house animals leaving the remaining floors for the humans. Like a small lighthouse, the stairways followed the curve of the walls. All five buildings featured lean-to additions which were usually occupied by the kitchen.

It is remarkable that all five structures have survived despite the abandonment of the Thames & Severn Canal. Today, four of the five buildings are occupied and they have all been treated in different ways.

Chalford Round House is well maintained and easy to see from the A419 road just below the church. After a spell as a small canal museum it became a private residence.

Above: Seen across the millpond of Belvedere Mill,
Chalford Round House in the early 1900s.
Below: Coates Round House in 2005

Coates Round House is the only derelict structure, now without its inverted roof but decay was halted by volunteers from the Cotswold Canals Trust some years ago. Its choked garden was cleared and dry stone boundary walls were rebuilt. Volunteers organise a regular clearance of the garden area. It faces an uncertain future, but a future all the same.

Cerney Wick Round House stands alongside the lock there by the road to the village whilst the one at Marston Meysey is harder to find. Many consider that the latter has been spoilt by its incorporation into a modern brick house in the 1980's, but better this than the previous dereliction.

Finally, Inglesham Round House stands alongside the Thames where the Thames & Severn Canal joins this Royal river. This building was bought by British Waterways when the organisation was lead partner of the Cotswold Canals Partnership. At the time of writing the round house was still owned by them and rented out to private tenants though it is not certain what the future ownership prospects are.

Cerney Wick Round House in 1985

Marston Meysey Round House in 1986 before a new structure was added

Inglesham Round House in the early 1900s

The Round House, Lechlade.

Brimscombe Port

Why is there a 'port' on a canal miles from the sea at Brimscombe? The answer is that this was not a conventional port but merely a point on the cross-country waterway route where the gauges of locks changed. This was a trans-shipment centre. Why Brimscombe? The location was chosen as the furthest point that Severn Trows could travel where there was sufficient room before the valley closed in.

The Stroudwater locks were built to accommodate Trows from the River Severn which were flat bottomed sailing vessels. Locks were around 16' wide and 70' long. The Thames & Severn adopted a gauge from Stroud to Brimscombe of 12' 9" wide by 74' and a longer 90' length between Brimscombe and the Thames to suit the dimensions of traffic expected from the river. This took account of the trans-shipment facilities at Brimscombe. Locks between there and Wildmoorway Lower Lock, near South Cerney, were shortened soon after the canal was opened to create the unique 'double top gate recesses'. With the motive of saving water, it is strange that this was done from the shallower top end.

The site was dominated by a large basin, around 700' long and 250' wide where loads were transferred from the Severn Trows to narrower Thames Barges or vice versa. Double handling was often necessary (together with port dues) when goods were stored on site between loads. The more valuable items such as coal could be left on the island site for security. Wharves and warehouses were built around the basin.

A boat weighing machine was installed which cradled the vessel to assess the toll that should be paid. It was dismantled in 1937 but a model can be found in the Gloucester Folk Museum. Midland narrow boats began to use the canal and because they fitted both sizes of locks had no need for trans-shipment facilities, but traffic using the whole route never came up to expectations anyway.

A large three storey building accommodated clerks for the Thames & Severn Canal Company as well as providing warehouse space. Gloucestershire County Council acquired the canal in the early 1900s and took the opportunity to convert this

A view from the island looking south-west towards Port Mill in the early 1900s

A view of the port looking north in the early 1900s

building into Brimscombe Polytechnic and it remained as a school until the early 1960s when it was demolished.

Due to an insufficient supply of small coins in the 1700s, a common practice was followed when half penny tokens were struck for the Thames & Severn Canal to pay the workforce. They were accepted in local shops and pubs, being ultimately 'payable at Brimscombe Port'.

Today only a few of the buildings associated with the site remain. In 1967 the basin was filled in and even the Polytechnic building was levelled to make way for modern factory units. This was a great loss coming so late just before interest in these canals revived. It only takes a visit to the popular renovated Gloucester Docks to see what could have been achieved here at Brimscombe Port.

Now, the port's future looks much brighter. Although the original line of the canal through the port is now used for car parking, the site has been purchased and will be developed with the restored canal at its heart when work to reopen the Thames & Severn Canal reaches Brimscombe.

The western entrance to Brimscombe Port in 2006 marked with the canal route.
1. Gough's Orchard Lock. 2. Site of Brimscombe Bridge.
3. The Ship Inn. 4. Site of the Canal Company HQ. 5. Salt warehouse.

Above: The old canal HQ shortly
before demolition in 1967
Below: An aerial view in 2006.
1. Port Mill.   2. Salt warehouse
3. Site of the Canal Company HQ
4. Site of the boat weighing machine.
5. Bourne Lock. 6. Position of the island wharf.

Both sides of
a canal token

Restoration

The two canals were officially abandoned between 1927 and 1954, but much of the damage was done in the 1960s before a restoration movement could promote their cause. In 1972, the Stroudwater Canal Society was formed but it was only in 1973 that a real start was made on improving the condition of the two waterways.

Ironically, the newly formed Stroudwater Canal Society made a start on the Thames & Severn Canal at Bowbridge. At that time, the Company of Proprietors of the Stroudwater Navigation were not sure that it was a good idea to let volunteers loose on the canal that they had built and still owned. Eventually, as the volunteers made their case and showed that they were serious, projects were allowed to be undertaken.

1. 1985 - Volunteers cleared the canal from Wallbridge to Bowbridge. Boat trips were operated on this section during the next year.

2. 1975 - Bowbridge Lock was at the western limit of the first restoration work.

3. 1982 - Cerney Wick Lock is cleared prior to repair of the walls.

4. 1984 - Volunteers restore Ryeford pedestrian swing-bridge.

5. 1986 - A job creation scheme at Ryeford dredged nearly a mile of canal.

6. 1986 - The same project. This is the disposal site for dredgings.

The Stroudwater Canal Society realised that restoration of both canals made more sense, so the organisation became the Stroudwater - Thames & Severn Canal Trust Ltd in 1975. By this time, the canal bed between Bowbridge and Thrupp had been transformed from a dry ditch, that was let out for grazing, back into a water channel maintained by concrete dams at locks.

Volunteers cleared and maintained towpaths and generally improved the condition of the canals working with tiny budgets. Numerous projects ensued but the three especially of note during the late 1970s and early 1980s were at Ryeford, Eastington and Cerney Wick.

Full engineering feasibility reports were prepared in the early 1990s and finally in 1996 Gloucestershire County Council commissioned British Waterways to prepare a 'corridor study' which would identify the economic benefits to the corridor through which the two waterways run. This study showed that both interim and full restoration would be very cost effective and create many new jobs in the canal corridor.

1. 1996 - Daneway Portal under restoration.

2. 1999 - The late Fred & Olive Bailey led the repair of Newtown Bridge.

3. 1992 - Gates are fitted to Blunder Lock, Eastington.

4. 1999 - WRG restore the towpath near South Cerney top lock.

5. 1999 - Stonehouse Bridge was built by Gloucestershire County Council during road realignment works, thereby removing a blockage.

6. 2000 - Celebrating completion of Stonehouse Bridge with the Cotswold Canals Trust's trip boat lifted by crane in to the section.

The role of the Trust in spearheading restoration has gradually changed with the lead now being taken by the restoration partnership. The Cotswold Canals Trust has considerable experience gained since 1972 and this knowledge has been imparted to the new partnership. There is still a vital political role to play in championing the restoration, promoting the canal both through the media, events and continuation of fund raising for restoration tasks within the Trust's volunteer capabilities.

Away from the major restoration projects, small groups of local and visiting volunteers work on restoration and maintenance often with little publicity.

In December 2008, after many months of work behind the scenes, Stroud District Council voted to become lead partner of the Cotswold Canals Partnership with help from the Cotswold Canals Trust. This unlocked the funding package to enable restoration of the 'Phase 1A' section of canal between Stonehouse and Brimscombe. Meanwhile other funding packages were sought to restore other sections of canal.

1. 2005 - Official 'opening' of Spine Road bridge in April.

2. 2005 - Pike road bridge, Eastington, formally opened in September.

3. 2003 - Early days during excavation of the infilled canal at Ebley.

4. 1992 - The infilled section at Ebley with volunteers controlling undergrowth.

5. 2007 - The same section at Ebley after excavation by developers.

6. 2008 - Oil Mills Bridge and canal, Ebley, reinstated removing another blockage.

Cotswold Canals Trust

On 12th May 1972, a meeting was held in Stroud Subscription Rooms to investigate the feasibility of restoring navigation on the Stroudwater Navigation, from its junction with the Gloucester/Sharpness Canal to Wallbridge, Stroud. This resulted in the formation of the 'Stroudwater Canal Society' which soon became the 'Stroudwater - Thames & Severn Canal Trust'. In 1990 the Trust announced that it was to adopt a new name - the 'Cotswold Canals Trust'.

The Cotswold Canals Trust has a vibrant and ever increasing membership (around 5,500 in 2009). Regular monthly social gatherings, canal based events and a quarterly magazine - *The Trow* - enable members to keep updated on the progress of restoration and to enjoy the canals.

'Armchair Members' are most welcome but those who want to take a more active role can choose from a wide variety of activities. Some enjoy helping to crew a trip boat, others like to man the publicity unit around the country. Of course many members enjoy restoring and maintaining the canal itself.

Why not join? Application forms are available wherever you see the Cotswold Canals Trust volunteers. Otherwise, contact details are:

44 Black Jack Street
Cirencester
Gloucestershire
GL7 2AA

Phone	**01285 643440**
email	**mail@cotswoldcanals.com**
website	**www.cotswoldcanals.com**

76

Above: Seen here at Crick Boat Show, the 'Roadshow' publicises the Trust locally and nationally.
Below: Trip boats crewed by volunteers attract visitors and raise funds.

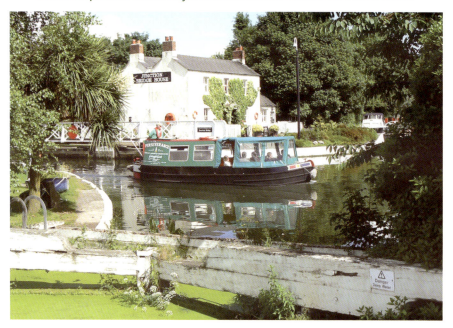

The Cotswold Canals Partnership

In July 2001, British Waterways and national charity The Waterways Trust published a feasibility report which led to the formation of the Cotswold Canals Partnership.

The aim of the partnership is to build on work achieved to date and deliver the full restoration of the Cotswold Canals.

The members of the partnership are:

The Waterways Trust
Cotswold Canals Trust
Stroud District Council
South West Regional Development Agency
Gloucestershire County Council
Wiltshire County Council
Gloucestershire First
Gloucestershire Rural Community Council
Environment Agency
Gloucestershire Soc for Industrial Archaeology
Learning & Skills Council
Cotswold Water Park Society
Inland Waterways Association
South West Tourism
Co. of Proprietors of the Stroudwater Navigation
North Wiltshire District Council
Cotswold District Council.

Prince Charles made his second visit to the Cotswold Canals in 2002 at the invitation of the Cotswold Canals Partnership - seen here by Coates Portal of Sapperton Tunnel.

The Cotswold Canals
LINKING THE THAMES AND SEVERN
Partnership
www.cotswoldcanalsproject.org

Representatives from these organisations belong to a project board which meets regularly to steer the project.

78

Further Reading

The two canals have been the subject of many publications over the years - the following list highlights the most popular. Those in **GREEN** are still available (as at January 2009) whilst those in **RED** are out of print but may often be found in second hand book shops or by searching the internet.

THE STROUDWATER NAVIGATION (Joan Tucker 2003)

THE STROUDWATER CANAL Vol 1 1729-1763 (M. Handford 1976 - early history)

THE STROUDWATER CANAL (Michael Handford 1979 - full history)

THE THAMES & SEVERN CANAL HISTORY & GUIDE (David Viner 2002)

THE THAMES & SEVERN CANAL (Humphrey Household 1969 to 1987)

THE THAMES & SEVERN CANAL (David Viner 1975 - historic photos)

AROUND THE COTSWOLD CANALS Vol 1 & 2 (Cotswold Canals Trust 1991 & after booklets about circular walks along and around the two canals)

STROUDWATER AND THAMES & SEVERN CANALS TOWPATH GUIDE
(Handford & Viner 1984 & 1988)

THE COTSWOLD CANALS WALK (Gerry Stewart 2000)

THE STROUDWATER and THAMES & SEVERN CANALS IN OLD PHOTOGRAPHS
(Edwin Cuss & Stanley Gardiner 1988,   A SECOND SELECTION 1993)

Further books about the Gloucester & Sharpness Canal and Gloucester Docks have been written by Hugh Conway-Jones.

Credits

Thank you to the following contributors who have allowed us to use their material in this book. Without them, its publication would not have been possible.

NICK BIRD

15a, 41b, 47a,47b, 51a, 51b, 55a, 56, 63b.
see his website at www.cotswoldcanals.net

PETER CHADWICK

59b, 64, 65a.

COTSWOLD CANALS TRUST ARCHIVE

11a, 11b, 53a, 58, 67b, 69a, 70.1, 70.2, 71.3, 71.4, 71.5, 71.6

SHIRLEY EASTO

(Loan of old postcards) Front Cover, 27b, 37b, 39a, 41a, 43a, 43b, 55b, 63a, 65b, 67a.

RICHARD FAIRHURST

Creation of Maps on pages 3,4,5,6,7

JACK FLEMONS

(Slides by the late Jack Flemons courtesy MICHAEL YOUNG - Thanks to MARK WELTON who converted the slides to digital images)13a, 15b, 31b, 60, 61a, 61b.

JEFF 'The Jar' **GILLMAN**

37a (loan of photo)

DAVID JOWETT

1, 13b, 17a, 17b, 19b, 21b. 23a, 23b, 25a, 25b, 29a, 29b, 33a, 33b, 35a, 35b, 45a, 49a, 49b, 53b, 57a, 57b, 59a, 72.2, 73.3, 73.4, 73.5, 73.6, 74.1, 74.2, 75,3, 75.4, 75.5, 75.6, 77a, 77b, Back Cover.

MAUREEN POULTON

72.1, 78

TOM ROUND-SMITH

45b.

STROUD DISTRICT COUNCIL &

(use of aerial photos) 19a, 21a, 27a, 31a, 39b, 68, 69b.

STROUD DISTRICT (COWLE) MUSEUM

9a, 9b.